Evanescence of Spring

Evanescence of Spring

Poems by

Nancy Dillingham

Cover art by Elizabeth Porritt Carrington, "The Gateway"
www.elizabethcarringtonart.com
Cover design by Shay Culligan
Author photo by Bill Mosher

ISBN: 978-1-63980-468-9

Kelsay Books
502 South 1040 East, A-119
American Fork, Utah 84003
Kelsaybooks.com

Contents

It is our inward journey that leads us through time—
forward or backward, seldom in a straight line,
most often spiraling.
—Eudora Welty

I

Love is like quicksilver in the hand.
—Dorothy Parker

The Ballad of Blossom and Frankie

Blossom lived with her mate
on a lake in Iowa near a cemetery

When Bud died
Blossom was lonely

staring at her own reflection
in gravestones and windowpanes

The general manager of the place
hatched a plan

ran a personal ad
that read

Lonely domestic goose
seeking partner
for companionship
and occasional shenanigans

Owners of a widower gander
named Frankie
arranged a blind date

At first glance
it was pure romance

They're together still today
staring at each other's faces

Deacon and Dancer

Our faces become our biographies.
—Cynthia Ozick

They grew up together in Plains
He wanted to marry her
after their first date

gave her a silver locket
engraved with "ILYTG"
their secret acronym

He served in the Navy
once dismantled
a damaged reactor

peed radioactive urine
for six months after

Known by the Secret Service
by the code names
Deacon and Dancer

she learned how to hula in Hawaii
and he taught Sunday School

He carried his own briefcase
and banned the playing
of "Hail to the Chief"

She championed mental health
and the Monarch butterfly

He won the Nobel Peace Prize

Eudora on the Porch

I see her now
like one of her own photographs

a shawl around her shoulders
a book in her lap

that high forehead
white hair
pin curled to the side

her voice
low and melodic

a chorus of words
coming from her mouth

In Search of Lost Time

*The true paradises
are the paradises we have lost.*
—Marcel Proust

She is there in the white corner cabinet
among graham crackers and spices

in the warming closet
of the wood-burning stove

in the homey aroma
of butter biscuits and corn pone

in the sharp tang
of the newspaper-lined pantry

filled with canning jars and pints
of vanilla-flavored pickled beets

tart and bittersweet

II

If we could light up the world with pain,
we'd be a glorious fire.
—Ada Limon

The Surgeon

First, do no harm.
　　—Hippocrates

The surgeon
enters the small
pre-op cubicle

stifles a yawn
drawls
Morning, y'all

begins his spiel
to the cadaver-like
patient

shrouded
in a metallic cap
and rattly paper gown

then asks
Any questions?

The patient rasps
Could I have a sip of water?

The surgeon
looking confused
responds

*The nurse
will get that for you*

then cap askew
exits the room

Butterfly

for Tyre Nichols
6/5/93–1/10/23

Police beat
the "impossibly thin" young man
lover of butterflies and sunsets

let him lie near death
for more than 22 minutes
before calling for help

cited him for reckless driving
but no record was kept

Members of the SCORPION elite
tased and pepper-sprayed him
kicked him in the face

beat him with a baton
betrayed him

He begged the cops
to stop
called for his mom

Five minutes from home
he lay splayed against a police car
while his mother felt his pain

Three days later
in the hospital he died

unrecognizable
his head the size of a watermelon
his neck and nose broken

Are Black youth
like the Monarch butterfly
a beautiful but endangered species?

Was his "crime"
being in the wrong place
at the wrong time

or just *being*?

Ruby Freeman

When Trump targeted
62-year-old election worker
Ruby Freeman
along with her daughter Shaye

made false claims of fraud
about ballots
in suitcases

they were inundated
with thousands of menacing
messages of hate

terrorist threats and racial slurs
calls for people to hurt
hang and behead them

Shouting MAGA crowds
surrounded Ruby's home
forcing her to flee

She called 911
Fulton County authorities
the FBI

asked for help
and a security detail
Officials denied her requests

When Ruby testified
before the January 6 committee
on live TV

She told how her son's struggles
her daughter's fears
her life on the run
took their toll

left her numb
When asked who she trusted
She replied *No one*

187 Minutes: Aftermath

Shrunken in his overcoat
"taxed and spent"
Trump at last
left the Oval
after watching hours
of Fox News
as his rabid gang
of rabble rousers
drunk on lies and power
stormed the Capitol
broke down barriers
assaulted the law
erected a noose for Pence
hunted down Pelosi
and other members
of Congress
in an attempt
to stop
the certification
of Biden's election
to the presidency

violence he instigated
and promulgated
before being pressured
to issue his directive
to the insurrectionists

Go home
We love you
You're very special

Cassidy Hutchinson: Portrait of a Patriot

Intimidated
called a traitor
a social climber
a leaker
a liar
a Total Phony

threatened with unemployment
betrayed by a lawyer
and her own father
who failed to support her

24-year-old Cassidy Hutchinson
former aide to Meadows
poised and unflappable
testified

recounted damning
accounts of conversations
in the White House

opened up and exposed
Trump's January 6
West Wing bunker

its ketchup-stained walls
and foot soldiers
dropped bombshells
and disclosed
incriminating details

Watching as rioters
erected gallows
defaced the Capitol
and shouted

Hang Mike Pence!
her trust
in the president
she once served
was shattered

I was disgusted
It was unpatriotic
she said

In that moment
doing what matters
what one is supposed to do—
tell the truth—

Cassidy Hutchinson
became an historic figure
and a true American hero

A Capitol Christmas

'Twas the night before Christmas
and all through the House
Nancy Pelosi was stirring—
she smelled a mouse

While children were nestled
all snug in their beds
her husband had been hammered
up side of the head

When out on the White House lawn
there came such a clatter
Biden sprang from his bed
to see what was the matter

And what to his wondering eyes should appear
but a bunch of Trumpers guided by fear
led by a blond-maned tyrant
in red tie and MAGA gear

who clapped and shouted
and called them by name

Come, Meadows! Come, Hawley!
Come Jordan and Greene
Come, Bannon! Come, Stone!

Let's bring down the House
and call it our home

But then in a twinkling
there came such a commotion
Joe in his nightcap
tired of the notion

More rapid than eagles
with courage they came
the hounds of democracy—
he called them by name

Now Thompson now Cheney
now Kinzinger and Schiff
now Ruskin now Lofgren—
you get the drift

With bundles of paper
they had flung on their backs
they looked just like prosecutors
as they opened their packs

They spoke not a word
but went straight to work
stuffing the stockings
their job not to shirk

The rioters were stunned
as they slunk out of sight
without one "Merry Christmas"
and nary a "Good Night"

Stormy Weather

I never lie.
—Stormy Daniels

As a young girl she loved horses
made straight *A*'s
dreamed of being a journalist

In 9th grade fear gripped her
she couldn't leave her seat
couldn't speak

took a zero
on an oral book report

At 17 she left home
became a stripper
named Stormy

enhanced her breasts
renamed them
Thunder and Lightning

became a porn star
and director

Namechecking an aggressor
became her claim
to fame

Though critics mocked her
many say her honesty
and moxie may well be

a bellwether
to dismantling a presidency
and saving democracy

Indictment in Manhattan

3/31/23

After a grand jury voted to indict
private citizen and twice-impeached
ex-president Donald J. Trump

he turned himself in
was arrested and arraigned
fingerprinted and Mirandized

The unsealed indictment
revealed 34 felony counts
for alleged shenanigans and crimes
related to the paying of hush money

to porn star Stormy Daniels
and Playmate Karen McDougal
in the "catch and kill" scheme

an illegal attempt to influence
the outcome of the 2016 election

While We Were Sleeping

4/16/23

Today the seeds of autocracy
planted by the ex-president
who made a mockery
of the rule of law
and democracy

were watered
and took hold
in Tennessee
where the GOP-
controlled legislature

expelled two young
Democratic Black men
for chanting too long
in the well

protesting lack of action
on gun violence
three days after
a mass shooting
in Nashville

When a white female
Dem who joined them
was asked how
she escaped expulsion

she spoke evoking
the specter of racism
*It might have had something
to do with the color of our skin*

The Slaughter of Cedar

4/4/23

Man's inhumanity to man
is only surpassed by his cruelty to animals.
— George Bernard Shaw

When a California mother
of a 9-year-old
caught her daughter
sobbing by the pen
of her pet goat Cedar

bought for a 4-H project
and scheduled for slaughter
she sought a reprieve
moved to rescue

Officers armed
with a judge's warrant
drove 500 miles
to retrieve the goat

took him back to Shasta County
to be auctioned off for meat
used for a communal barbeque

III

We are the breakers of our own hearts.
—Eudora Welty

Billie Holiday Sang the Blues

in beautiful honeyed tones
Good morning, heartache
What's new?

in a plaintive voice
like a little girl
full of sadness and woe

conveying innocence
and life-weariness
at the same time

like a waif
on a street corner
begging for a dime

Nina Simone: High Priestess of Soul

Eunice Kathleen Waymon
reinvented herself
as Nina Simone
composed her most
well-known anthem
"Mississippi Goddam"

to protest the murders
of Medgar Evers
and 4 little black girls
in a church bombing in Birmingham

Blacklisted by record companies
and refused concert venues
she sought refuge outside the US
settled in France

Denied permission
to the Curtis Institute
of Music

she was awarded
an honorary degree
by the school
2 days before her death

Her hometown of Tryon
erected an 8-foot likeness of her
and welded part of her ashes
into the sculpture's heart

Iris DeMent's Lament

Singing is praying.

Armed with her musical arsenal
her pumping upright piano
and idiosyncratic phrasing
the Arkansas-born folk artist
vents her pent-up frustrations
about the sociopolitical state
of our nation today

In an 8-minute anthem
sparked with sass and sarcasm
she fires off a salvo of complaints

I'm goin' down to sing in Texas
where anybody can carry a gun

and with false bravado
issues a taunt

Go ahead and shoot me
if it floats your little boat

allowing
with bittersweet irony
that she is only a pilgrim
passing through
and like her heroes
John Lewis and Rachel Corrie
can never say

how her working on a world
may play

Van Gogh on Fire

Sadness will last forever.
—Vincent van Gogh's last words

The same glow
that lights up sunflowers
and starry nights

and burns gold
across wheat fields
like wild fire

inflamed his brain
his emotions
tortured his soul

Vermeer: Painter of *Girl with the Pearl Earring*

Unable to sell
his paintings

he fell
into "decadency and decay"

one day healthy
next day dead

After his death
his wife
traded his art for bread

Accidental Pilgrim

I can, with one eye squinted,
take it all as a blessing.

Devotees and fans of Flannery O'Connor
make annual pilgrimages
to the cemetery in Milledgeville

leave their pain and mementos
peacock feathers and rosaries
at her flat gravestone

like the writer
on her lone trip to Lourdes
dipping in the waters of the shrine
seeking healing for crumbling bones

IV

Every morning the world is created.
    —Mary Oliver

After Rain:

a spider web
atop boxwood
white lace
dew-laden

an elegant blue jay
in bas-relief
against a bay windowpane

blossom-shaped clouds
bowed
under their own weight

juxtaposed
against blue mountain
shoulders

a fog face
a rainbow

Still Life

Mountain's blue bowl
holds an evergreen frieze

glowed to sheen
by the hard bold cold
of a frozen morning

Light Show

. . . all else melted away.
—Rumi

As the earths turns
far-flung stars

like rich seasoning
salt the sky

The Evanescence of Spring

On a windswept day of false spring
daffodils in the open field
propose their golden blossoming

buds brimming
with hope and possibility

Then the snow comes
weighty and intimidating
filling up their yellow cups

The next day
the air warms
and the snow vanishes

giving way to the evanescence
of swaying flowers
doing their riotous dance

taking their chances
melting winter away

About the Author

Nancy Dillingham is a sixth-generation Dillingham from the small community of Dillingham in Big Ivy in western North Carolina. Her poetry, short fiction, and commentary have appeared in various venues.

She is associate editor of the online poetry journal *Speckled Trout Review* and coeditor of four anthologies of western North Carolina women writers. Her poetry collection *Home* was nominated for a SIBA, and her most recent publication is the chapbook *A Wild Shining.*

She resides in Asheville, NC.

www.ingramcontent.com/pod-product-compliance
Lightning Source LLC
Chambersburg PA
CBHW031008090426
42737CB00008B/733